Circus Fun

Dona Herweck Rice

Publishing Credits

Rachelle Cracchiolo, M.S.Ed., *Publisher*
Conni Medina, M.A.Ed., *Managing Editor*
Nika Fabienke, Ed.D., *Content Director*
Véronique Bos, *Creative Director*
Shaun N. Bernadou, *Art Director*
Carol Huey-Gatewood, M.A.Ed., *Editor*
John Leach, *Assistant Editor*
Courtney Roberson, *Senior Graphic Designer*

Image Credits: p.9 (top) Natursports/Shutterstock; All other images from iStock and/or Shutterstock.

Teacher Created Materials
5301 Oceanus Drive
Huntington Beach, CA 92649-1030
www.tcmpub.com

ISBN 978-1-4938-9854-1

Printed in China
Nordica.082018.CA21800936

We will see a 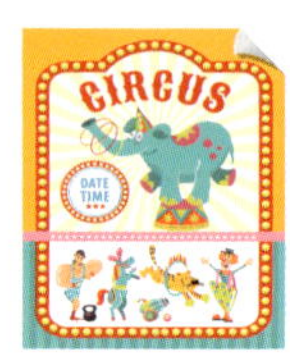

poster ,

not a 
painting .

We will see a 

,

ticket

not a  .

book

We will see a  ,

tent

not a  .

school

We will see a  magician,

not a  doctor.

We will see a ,

ring

not a .

square

We will see a  ,

unicycle

not a  .

wagon

We will see a  ,

corn dog

not a  .

cake

We will see a  juggler,

not a  soccer player.

We will see a  clown,

not a  teacher.

We will see a  ,

trapeze

not a  .

slide

High-Frequency Words

New Words

not see
we will

Review Word

a